Where We Live

Italy

Donna Bailey and Anna Sproule

STECK-VAUGHN
L I B R A R Y
A Division of Steck-Vaughn Company

Hello. My name is Laura, and these are my friends.
Maria is on my right, and Anna, Paola, and
Lucia are on my left.
We all live in Venice.

Venice is a city by the sea in northern Italy.
It is built on 118 little islands
in a lagoon.

In Venice, there are canals between
the houses instead of roads.
People travel around the city in boats
such as water buses and water taxis.

My father has a restaurant
by one of the canals.
In the summer the tourists sit outside
and eat beside the canal.

Mom and my aunt cook the food in the kitchen.
They make special Venetian dishes.
People in northern Italy eat a lot of rice,
so my aunt is cooking a huge pan of rice.

Every morning Mom goes to the market to buy fresh meat and vegetables for the restaurant.
She travels in a ferry called a "traghetto."

In the center of Venice is a big market where Mom buys fish, meat, fruit, and vegetables. People in Italy like to buy fresh food every day.

Boxes of fresh fruit and vegetables from
the countryside near Venice are brought
to the market on boats.
The men unload the boats and wheel the
boxes on their carts to the market stalls.

9

Other boats deliver huge jugs of wine
and cases of soft drinks to
my father's restaurant.

10

People put their trash out
beside the canals.
The trash collectors load it
into their boat.

In some of the smaller canals,
the boats are almost too big
to get under the low bridges.

The most famous boats in Venice
are the gondolas.
Many gondoliers wear striped shirts.
They row tourists around the city
to see the famous bridges and palaces.

The gondoliers wait for tourists by
the steps near St. Mark's Square.
St. Mark's Square is the
most famous square in Venice.

14

Tourists like to sit outside the restaurants
in St. Mark's Square.
They listen to musicians playing songs and
watch the children feeding the pigeons.

When it rains in the winter, the canals
sometimes overflow their banks.
Then the water floods into St. Mark's Square,
and people walk on wooden platforms
to keep their feet dry.
Venice is famous for its canals and
its beauty.

In late summer, people watch
the annual Regatta.
The Regatta starts with a parade of
decorated boats along the Grand Canal.
After the parade there are boat races.
It is very exciting to watch.

The Regatta in Venice takes place in
early September.
People start to get ready for it
long before that.
The gondoliers take their boats out of
the water to paint and decorate them.

Some gondoliers paint their boats with
gold paint and put brightly-colored
cushions in them.

The teams of gondoliers who row these boats all wear shirts of the same color.

The bigger boats have carved animals
in the front.
The boat in this picture has a dragon.
Can you see the boat with
the galloping horses?

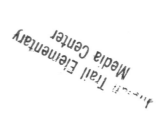

Other gondoliers put flags over their boats.
Their passengers wear costumes that
were worn long ago in Venice.

This big boat is a special barge.
The trumpeters at the front of the barge
play their trumpets, and the rowers
all wear gold jackets.

When the Regatta begins, the barge and
all the other boats row in a parade
along the Grand Canal.

Everyone in Venice comes to watch the parade.
Some people crowd into boats at the side
of the canal.

People cheer and wave at their friends and relatives in the boats.

Other people crowd onto balconies and
lean out of windows to watch the parade.

Crowds of people stand at the water's edge
near St. Mark's Square to see the boats.

After the parade the teams of gondoliers
get ready for the races.
They row to the starting point and
wait for the starting signal.

When the signal comes to start
each race, the teams speed
along the Grand Canal.

Gondoliers do not row facing backward,
as most people do.
They stand up in the boat and face forward.
They row as hard as they can
to the finish line.

The races are very exciting to watch.
The boats speed through the water.
People cheer their favorite team and hope
it will win a prize in the Venice Regatta.